First World War
and Army of Occupation
War Diary
France, Belgium and Germany

57 DIVISION
170 Infantry Brigade
Loyal North Lancashire Regiment
4/5th Battalion (Territorial Force)
11 February 1917 - 31 January 1918

WO95/2979/5

The Naval & Military Press Ltd
www.nmarchive.com
Published in association with The National Archives

Published by

The Naval & Military Press Ltd

Unit 10 Ridgewood Industrial Park,

Uckfield, East Sussex,

TN22 5QE England

Tel: +44 (0) 1825 749494

www.naval-military-press.com

www.nmarchive.com

This diary has been reprinted in facsimile from the original. Any imperfections are inevitably reproduced and the quality may fall short of modern type and cartographic standards.

© Crown Copyright
Images reproduced by permission of The National Archives, London, England, 2015.

Contents

Document type	Place/Title	Date From	Date To
Heading	WO95/2979-5		
Heading	War Diary Of 4/5th Bn. Loyal North Lancashire Regt From 11th February 1917 To 28th February 1917 (Volume I)		
War Diary	Blackdown	11/02/1917	11/02/1917
War Diary	Folkestone	12/02/1917	12/02/1917
War Diary	Boulogne	12/02/1917	14/02/1917
War Diary	Outtersteene	14/02/1917	18/02/1917
War Diary	Rouge-De-Bout	19/02/1917	23/02/1917
War Diary	Trenches	24/02/1917	28/02/1917
Miscellaneous	D.A.G 3rd Echelon	02/04/1917	02/04/1917
Heading	War Diary Of 4/5th Bn. Loyal North Lancashire Regiment From 1st March 1917 To 31st March 1917		
War Diary	Trenches	01/03/1917	03/03/1917
War Diary	Billets	04/03/1917	09/03/1917
War Diary	Trenches	10/03/1917	15/03/1917
War Diary	Fleurbaix	16/03/1917	23/03/1917
War Diary	Trenches	24/03/1917	31/03/1917
Heading	War Diary Of 4/5th Bn. Loyal North Lancashire Regiment From 1st April 1917 To 30th April 1917 Volume 3		
War Diary	Fleurbaix	01/04/1917	30/04/1917
Heading	War Diary Of 4/5th Bn. Loyal North Lancashire Regiment From 1st May 1917 To 31st May 1917 Volume 4		
War Diary	Fleurbaix	01/05/1917	31/05/1917
Miscellaneous	Herewith War Diary For The Battalion under my Command covering period 1/6/1917 To 30/6/1917	01/07/1917	01/07/1917
Heading	War Diary Of 4/5th Bn. Loyal North Lancashire Regiment From 1st June 1917 To 30th June 1917 Volume 5		
War Diary	Boutillerie Sub-Sector	01/06/1917	02/06/1917
War Diary	Fleurbaix	03/06/1917	10/06/1917
War Diary	Boutillerie Sub-Sector	11/06/1917	17/06/1917
War Diary	Fleurbaix	18/06/1917	25/06/1917
War Diary	Boutillerie Sub-Sector	26/06/1917	30/06/1917
Heading	War Diary Of 4/5th Bn. Loyal North Lancashire Regiment From 1st July 1917 To 31st July 1917 Volume 6		
War Diary	Fleurbaix	01/07/1917	06/07/1917
War Diary	Boutillerie Sub-Sector	06/07/1917	15/07/1917
War Diary	Fleurbaix	16/07/1917	22/07/1917
War Diary	Boutillerie Sub-Sector	23/07/1917	31/07/1917
Miscellaneous	Headquarters 57th Division	01/09/1917	01/09/1917
Heading	War Diary Of 4/5th Battalion Loyal North Lancashire Regiment From 1st August 1917 To 31st August 1917 Volume 7		
War Diary	Boutillerie Sub-Sector	01/08/1917	01/08/1917
War Diary	Fleurbaix	02/08/1917	02/08/1917
War Diary	Armentieres	03/08/1917	09/08/1917

War Diary	Houplines	10/08/1917	18/08/1917
War Diary	Armentieres	19/08/1917	26/08/1917
War Diary	Houplines	27/08/1917	31/08/1917
Miscellaneous	Headquarters 57th Division	02/10/1917	02/10/1917
Heading	War Diary Of 4/5th Battalion Loyal North Lancashire Regiment From 1st September 1917 To 30th September 1917 Volume 8		
War Diary	Houplines	01/09/1917	03/09/1917
War Diary	Armentieres	04/09/1917	11/09/1917
War Diary	Houplines	11/09/1917	16/09/1917
War Diary	Waterlands	17/09/1917	18/09/1917
War Diary	Neuf Berquin	19/09/1917	19/09/1917
War Diary	La Pierriere	20/09/1917	20/09/1917
War Diary	Rely	21/09/1917	30/09/1917
Heading	War Diary Of 4/5th Battalion Loyal North Lancashire Regiment From 1st October 1917 To 31st October 1917 Volume 9		
War Diary	Rely	01/10/1917	16/10/1917
War Diary	Campagne	17/10/1917	17/10/1917
War Diary	Proven	18/10/1917	24/10/1917
War Diary	Front Line	25/10/1917	27/10/1917
War Diary	Proven	28/10/1917	31/10/1917
Operation(al) Order(s)	170th Inf. Bde. Order No. 92	24/10/1917	24/10/1917
Miscellaneous	Signalling Communications		
Miscellaneous	Disposal Of Prisoners During Operations		
Miscellaneous	Report Upon Attack Made By The 4/5th Bn. Loyal North Lancashire Regt.	26/10/1917	26/10/1917
Miscellaneous	170th Infantry Brigade	28/10/1917	28/10/1917
Map	Map		
Miscellaneous	Message Pad		
Miscellaneous	Headquarters 57th Division	30/11/1917	30/11/1917
War Diary	Proven	01/11/1917	08/11/1917
War Diary	Licques	09/11/1917	30/11/1917
Miscellaneous	Extract From 57th (West Lancs.) Divisional Routine Order No. 1754	27/11/1917	27/11/1917
Miscellaneous	Headquarters 57th Division	01/01/1918	01/01/1918
Heading	War Diary Of 4/5th Battalion Loyal North Lancashire Regiment From 1st December 1917 To 31st December 1917 Volume II		
War Diary	Licques	01/12/1917	09/12/1917
War Diary	Proven	10/12/1917	13/12/1917
War Diary	Rousbrugge Haringhe	14/12/1917	16/12/1917
War Diary	Woeston	17/12/1917	28/12/1917
War Diary	De Wippe Woeston	29/12/1917	31/12/1917
Miscellaneous	Herewith War Diary Of The Unit Under My Command period 1st To 31st January 1918	01/02/1918	01/02/1918
Heading	War Diary Of 4/5th Battalion Loyal North Lancashire Regiments From 1st January 1918 To 31st January 1918 Volume 12		
War Diary	Proven	01/01/1918	02/01/1918
War Diary	Steenwerck	03/01/1918	03/01/1918
War Diary	Erquinghem	04/01/1918	09/01/1918
War Diary	Chapelle Sector	10/01/1918	13/01/1918
War Diary	Name Of Sector Changed To Wez Macquart	13/01/1918	13/01/1918
War Diary	Wez Macquart Sector	14/01/1918	15/01/1918
War Diary	Erquinghem	16/01/1918	19/01/1918

War Diary	Wez Macquart	20/01/1918	22/01/1918
War Diary	Erquinghem	23/01/1918	25/01/1918
War Diary	Wez Macquart	26/01/1918	28/01/1918
War Diary	Erquinghem	28/01/1918	31/01/1918
Heading	57th Division 170th Infy Bde 2-5th Bn K.O.R.O.Y. Lancaster Regt. 1915 Aug-1916 Feb And 1917 Feb-1918 Mar And 1919 Jan-1919 May		

WO 05/30679

WO 05/2979 (5)

Vol I

Confidential

War Diary
of
1/5th Bn. Royal North Lancashire Regt.
from 11th February 1917. to 28th February 1917.
(Volume I)

WAR DIARY or INTELLIGENCE SUMMARY

Army Form C. 2118

(Erase heading not required.)

Place	Date	Hour	Summary of Events and Information	Remarks and references to Appendices
BLACKDOWN	11-2-17	11:30 AM	Left BLACKDOWN. Entrained at FARNBOROUGH. S.E.C.R. for FOLKESTONE. Strength 24 Officers 826 O'Ranks.	B.N.R.
FOLKESTONE	12-2-17	6 AM	Arrived SHORNCLIFFE. Rest camp FOLKESTONE. Embarked 3 PM for BOULOGNE.	B.N.R.
BOULOGNE	12-2-17	5:15 PM	Arrived. Marched to OSTROHOVE rest camp. Spent night there.	B.N.R.
"	13-2-17	—	OSTROHOVE rest camp.	B.N.R.
"	14-2-17	7:15 AM	Marched out. Entrained 9 AM for "Concentration area."	B.N.R.
OUTTERSTEENE	14-2-17	10:45 AM	Arrived. Battalion billeted for the night. Casualties to date NIL.	B.N.R.
"	15-2-17	—	Transport section arrived via HAVRE. 10:30 AM. Strength 3 Officers, 82 O'Ranks. Total 27 Officers 908 O'Ranks.	B.N.R.
"	16-2-17	—	Billets.	B.N.R.
"	17-2-17	—	Billets.	B.N.R.
"	18-2-17	—	Left OUTTERSTEENE. 9 AM. Marched to ROUGE de BOUT, in billets as Brigade Reserve.	B.N.R.
ROUGE-de-BOUT	19-2-17	—	Brigade Reserve Billets. "A" Coy advanced party proceeded to trenches. Officers N.C.O. men of advanced party reported.	B.N.R.
"	20-2-17	—	Brigade Reserve Billets. "C" Coy advanced party proceeded to trenches. Capt. Kipping reported from HAVRE.	B.N.R.
"	21-2-17	—	Brigade Reserve Billets. "B" Coy advanced party proceeded to trenches.	B.N.R.
"	22-2-17	—	Brigade Reserve Billets. "C" Coy relieved "B" Coy of 2/4 R.N.R. in front line trenches. "D" Coy advanced party proceeded to trenches.	B.N.R.
"	23-2-17	—	Brigade Reserve Billets. "B" Coy relieved "A" Coy 2/4 R.N.R. Reg. in front line trenches. "A" Coy advanced party proceeded to trenches.	B.N.R.
Trenches.	24-2-17	.	Bn. H.Qrs. relieved Bn. H.Qrs. 2/4" L.N.L Regt. "D" Coy relieved "C" Coy 2/4" R.N.L Regt. Situation Normal. Enemy's artillery head in enemy front line. Quiet day.	B.N.R.
"	25-2-17	.	"A" Coy relieved "D" Coy 2/4 R.N.L Regt. Both relief complete. Enemy's Day. Enemy artillery inactive. Our artillery + T.M.B. shelled enemy positions intermittently during the day.	B.N.R.
"	26-2-17	.	Trenches. Our artillery active. Casualties: Killed 1 wounded 3 (i.Coy 3, D.Coy 1). Patrol visited enemy wire in front of own left Coy reported all quiet in front trenches. Heavy barrage S. The N. of our trenches at 9.45 & 10.15 PM. & again from midnight to 12.30 AM.	B.N.R.

Army Form C. 2118

WAR DIARY
or
INTELLIGENCE SUMMARY
(Erase heading not required.)

Instructions regarding War Diaries and Intelligence Summaries are contained in F.S. Regs., Part II. and the Staff Manual respectively. Title Pages will be prepared in manuscript.

Place	Date	Hour	Summary of Events and Information	Remarks and references to Appendices
Trenches.	27/2/17	-	Situation normal. Very quiet day. Enemy refrained from shelling our trenches. Occasional indirect M.G. fire in neighbohood of Batn H.Qrs. Casualties. Nil.	A.N.N.-
-"-	28/2/17	-	Situation normal. Nothing to report.	B.N.N.-

Colbert Maxford
Lieut. Colonel,
Comdg. 4/5 Loyal North Lanc. Regt.

CONFIDENTIAL

D.A.G.,
3rd Echelon.

    Herewith War Diary of the Battalion under my Command for period commencing 1st March 1917 and finishing on the 31st March 1917, please.

C. Lloyd Harford

3/4/1917.

Lieut-Col.,
Comdg. 4/5th Bn. L. N. Lancashire Regt.

Vol 2 57

Confidential

War Diary
of
1/5th Bn. Royal North Lancashire Regiment

From 1st March 1917 to 31st March 1917.

Army Form C. 2118

WAR DIARY
or
INTELLIGENCE SUMMARY

(Erase heading not required.)

Instructions regarding War Diaries and Intelligence Summaries are contained in F.S. Regs., Part II. and the Staff Manual respectively. Title Pages will be prepared in manuscript.

Place	Date	Hour	Summary of Events and Information	Remarks and references to Appendices
TRENCHES	1-3-17	—	Situation normal. Casualties 1.N.C.O. wounded. Patrol visited enemy wire in front of left sub-sector, reports all quiet in enemy line. A patrol of 1 officer + 3.O.R. entered enemy line in front of right sub-sector. Enemy trenches reported in bad condition, front line very weakly held.	B.H.Q.
—"—	2-3-17	—	Situation normal. Artillery on both sides very quiet. A patrol of 5 N.C.O men under 2 Lieut. G. GREEN entered enemy front line opposite our right sub-sector, and patrolled their trenches for distance of 150 yards. No enemy sentries or patrols were encountered. "Stick" hand grenades were found on enemy parapets in great condition & apparently of recent issue. Men were brought back. Enemy first line trenches were reported 5ft. 6in. in a very bad state of repair.	B.H.Q.
—"—	3-3-17	—	Situation normal. Battalion relieved by 2/4 N.Z. Regt, & returned to billets near ROUGE-de-BOUT at 11.P.M.	B.H.Q.
BILLETS	4-3-17		Day spent in resting, men cleaning up	B.H.Q.
—"—	5-3-17		Training. Working Parties & Baths.	B.H.Q.
—"—	6-3-17		Training. Working Parties & Baths.	B.H.Q.
—"—	7-3-17		Training. Working Parties & Baths.	B.H.Q.
—"—	8-3-17		Battalion moved to FLEURBAIX billets.	B.H.Q.
—"—	9-3-17		Relieved 2/8 "King's" Liverpool Regt. in trenches, relief complete at 11.30 A.M. Situation normal. Listening patrols reported all quiet on our front during the night.	B.H.Q.

Army Form C. 2118

WAR DIARY
or
INTELLIGENCE SUMMARY

(Erase heading not required.)

Instructions regarding War Diaries and Intelligence Summaries are contained in F. S. Regs., Part II. and the Staff Manual respectively. Title Pages will be prepared in manuscript.

Place	Date	Hour	Summary of Events and Information	Remarks and references to Appendices
TRENCHES	10-3-17	—	Morning situation normal. Enemy machine guns very active on our parapet. Communication trenches from 6 P.M. onwards.	
		6.30 – 9.30 P.M.	35 rifle grenades landed in centre sector. Machine guns still active.	
		9.45 P.M.	Enemy opened heavy bombardment on centre support line. Rifle & left companies shelled both firing & support line.	R.N.N.
		9.50 P.M.	Enemy bombardment increased. S.O.S. sent by flare which our artillery replied promptly.	
		10.20 P.M.	Enemy artillery ceased fire. Support Company came up & reinforce centre coy. 9.00 or more reported approaching left company front.	
		10.27 P.M.	Our artillery ceased fire.	
		10.50 P.M.	Situation normal. Subsidiary Company returned to hut. A raid into enemy's entrenched line was frustrated by the bomb reserve from artillery. During the night two hostile patrols were located at our wire which dispersed by Lewis guns & Bomb. Casualties 1 man wounded.	
TRENCHES	11-3-17	12.30 A.M.	Enemy sent 6 & 8 guns shells behind centre support line. Necessary precaution were taken. Remainder of day situation normal. Enemy artillery Machine Guns very quiet.	R.N.N.
TRENCHES	12-3-17		Quiet day. 23 minnies on centre sector front line. Considerable material damage done. Enemy artillery very quiet & guns quiet. Casualties 4 NCO men wounded.	R.N.N.

Army Form C. 2118

WAR DIARY
or
INTELLIGENCE SUMMARY
(Erase heading not required.)

Instructions regarding War Diaries and Intelligence Summaries are contained in F. S. Regs., Part II. and the Staff Manual respectively. Title Pages will be prepared in manuscript.

Place	Date	Hour	Summary of Events and Information	Remarks and references to Appendices
TRENCHES	13-3-17	—	Situation normal. Enemy front line support line heavily bombarded from 4.30 PM to 4.50 PM by 18 pdrs & 4.5" Howitzers. Practice barrage + artillery raid. Trenches in bad state owing to wet weather. Enemy artillery machine guns quiet.	R.W.H
TRENCHES	14-3-17	—	Situation normal. Our artillery active all day, to which the enemy replied at intervals on various parts of our line. Capt. G.B. Hill and 14 O.Ranks wounded whilst firing rifle grenade battery at about 10.30 PM, presumably by enemy rifle grenade dropping amongst them.	R.N.H
TRENCHES	15-3-17	—	Situation normal. Enemy artillery active during afternoon, about 200 5.9 HE were fired at our right subsector. Mostly overshooting. Damage slight. Casualties NIL. Battalion relieved by 2/5 King's Own R.L. Regt in the evening, relief complete 9.12 PM, when the battalion proceeded to billets in FLEURBAIX.	R.N.H
FLEURBAIX	16-3-17	—	Billets. Nothing to report.	R.N.H
"	17-3-17	—	Billets. Working Parties. Baths. Training.	R.N.H
"	18-3-17	—	Billets. Working Parties. Baths. Training.	R.N.H
"	19-3-17	—	Billets. Working Parties. Training.	R.N.H
"	20-3-17	—	Billets. Working Parties. Training.	R.N.H
"	21-3-17	—	Billets. Working Parties. Training. Baths.	R.N.H
"	22-3-17	—	Billets. Working Parties. Training. Baths.	R.N.H
"	23-3-17	—	Left Billets 6.15 PM to relieve 2/5 Bn "King's Own" R.L. Regt. Relief complete 8.27 PM. Quiet night, no hostile artillery or M.G. activity. Arrival parties went up from Enemy front line.	R.N.H

WAR DIARY or INTELLIGENCE SUMMARY

Army Form C. 2118

Place	Date	Hour	Summary of Events and Information	Remarks and references to Appendices
TRENCHES	24-3-17	–	Situation normal. Usual "Minnies" on salient. 1 O.R. killed by Whizz-bang.	B.M.B.
–"–	25-3-17	–	Situation normal. During afternoon "Minnies" very active in salient + our wire in front of it. Casualties NIL.	B.M.B
–"–	26-3-17	–	Enemy artillery active all day, about 30 "Minnies", "73" whizz bang + about 40 H.E. were fired on our centre sub-sector during the afternoon – our 18 Pdrs + 60 Pdrs replied on enemy support line; enemy sent a further 20 H.E. over after which his artillery was quiet. Few rifle grenades in our front line during the night. Three patrols went out during the night as follows:- 1. One Officer (2 Lt J.C. CICERI) + two O.R. left our trenches, no German sub-sectors at 1 A.M. + succeeded in reaching enemy trench of which 150 yards were traversed, enemy front line reported to be practically obliterated, very lights were being sent up from his half front line. Patrol returned at 4 A.M. without having come in contact with enemy. 2. Lieut J.A.TILL + 2 O.R. left our trenches, no. 8 sub-sector, at 1.5 A.M. Patrol succeeded in getting to within 30 yards of enemy front line. Two sentries located one in No Mans Land, one in enemy front line. Patrol was held stationary by a party being pushed along tramline. Very lights were sent up from enemy support line. Patrol did not reach enemy wire as they were fired on by enemy sniper. Patrol returned at 3.10 A.M. firing in No Mans Land heard. 3. Lieut H.B. MONEY + 2 O.R. left our centre sub-sector at 11.15 P.M. Too dark to see enemy wire. Progress barred by ditch 30 to 40 yards from enemy front line – nothing seen or heard in front. Very light afterwards fired from relieved enemy front line.	R.M.H.
–"–	27-3-17	–	Situation normal. Generally quiet. Enemy active during afternoon with Rover Minnies various calibres. To silent our howitzers replied with his on enemy support trenches – Night fairly quiet. A patrol of 6 O.R. under C.S.M. BRABIN Over	

WAR DIARY or INTELLIGENCE SUMMARY

Army Form C. 2118

Place	Date	Hour	Summary of Events and Information	Remarks and references to Appendices
TRENCHES	27.3.17	—	Patrol left our centre sub-sector at 12.10 A.M. & succeeded in reaching enemy trenches at 12.45 A.M. Patrol waited for an hour when a hostile patrol of 10 men were seen getting over their parapet about 15 yards to the left. Patrol then retired about 30 yards & lie in wait for enemy, when they were seen by enemy sentry & very light went up, followed by rifle grenades, machine gun rifle & M.G. fire. Two men were wounded, one 2/Lt. NETHERS (who he was carried back to our trenches under heavy fire) by C.S.M. BRABIN. Patrol reported enemy wire bad & easy to get through.	R.N.H.
"	28.3.17	—	Day generally quiet. Enemy sent over 42 "Minnies" during the afternoon. These were replied to by our Artillery, & 60 Trench Mortars. A patrol from our centre sub-sector went out at 10.45 P.M., reached enemy line, waited for 45 minutes, during which no enemy was seen & hand patrol returned at 1 A.M.	R.N.H.
"	29.3.17	—	Situation normal. Nothing to report. Draft of 46 O.R. arrived from 8 Bn. L.N.L.Rgt. Usual "Minnies" on centre sub-sector.	R.N.H.
"	30.3.17	—	"Minnies" on centre sub-sector active in afternoon. Our 60 lbs & 4.5" Howitzers replied & effectually silenced the Minnenwerfer. Several direct hits on the Emplacements were claimed. Night was quiet, patrols listening posts report enemy quiet.	R.N.H.
"	31.3.17	—	Very quiet. Enemy artillery especially so. No "Minnies" on centre sub-sector. Emplacements believed to have been destroyed as results of previous day's bombardment. Battalion was relieved by the Finsburys by the 2/5 Gen. Kings Own R.L.Rgt. Relief completed at 10.50 P.M. when battalion marched to billets in FLEUR BAIX.	R.N.H.

"Confidential."

War Diary
of
1/5th Bn. Royal Irish Lancashire Regiment
from 1st April 1917 to 30th April 1917.

Volume 3

Army Form C. 2118

WAR DIARY
or
INTELLIGENCE SUMMARY
(Erase heading not required.)

Instructions regarding War Diaries and Intelligence Summaries are contained in F.S. Regs., Part II. and the Staff Manual respectively. Title Pages will be prepared in manuscript.

Place	Date	Hour	Summary of Events and Information	Remarks and references to Appendices
FLEURBAIX	1-4-17	—	Billets resting. A Special Patrol of 2 Lieut. G. GREEN & 4 O. Ranks proceeded to trenches. Patrol went out from Centre Sub-Sector with the object of locating Sentry groups in enemy front line in vicinity of CORNER FORT. Patrol succeeded in reaching enemy front line & located a sentry group on either side of spot reached about 100 yards apart. Passage through enemy wire was considerably helped by a snowstorm, which subsequently cleared & made proper enemy front line impossible. As this junctive patrol was spotted & fired with rifle & machine guns, patrol lay still for half an hour & no firing both continued decided to return to our trenches which were reached without any casualties being sustained. Patrol was out from 9 P.M. 1-4-17 until 2 A.M. 2-4-17.	R.N.H.
"	2-4-17	—	Billets. Working parties. Training. Baths. Working parties in the evening. Carried usual carry on with work on account of frost.	R.N.H.
"	3-4-17	—	Billets. Working parties (evening) training & baths. Morning working parties unable to work on account of snow.	R.N.H.
"	4-4-17	—	Billets. Working parties. Training. Baths.	R.N.H.
"	5-4-17	—	Billets. Working parties. Training. Baths.	R.N.H.
"	6-4-17	—	Billets. Working parties. Training. Baths.	R.N.H.

Army Form C. 2118

WAR DIARY
or
INTELLIGENCE SUMMARY

(Erase heading not required.)

Instructions regarding War Diaries and Intelligence Summaries are contained in F.S. Regs., Part II. and the Staff Manual respectively. Title Pages will be prepared in manuscript.

Place	Date	Hour	Summary of Events and Information	Remarks and references to Appendices
FLEURBAIX	7-4-17	-	Billets. Working Parties. Battn. Training	B.N.H.
"	8-4-17	-	Battalion Inspected by G.O.C. 140th Infantry Brigade. Battalion relieved 2/5th Battn. Kings Own R.L. Regt. Reliefs FLEURBAIX at 6 P.M. relief complete at 10.30 P.M. Night quiet. Patrolling impossible owing to bright moon & exceptionally clear night.	B.N.H.
"	9-4-17	-	Quiet day. 36 whizz bangs & 6 medium "minnies" in Centre Subsector. A patrol of 3.O.R. under Lieut. J.A. Tice went out from LEFT subsector, reported all quiet in enemy lines. Lieut. C.G. Hein & 3.O.R. went out from RIGHT subsector, reported all quiet. No sign of enemy. Party in No Mans Land fair. Both patrols went out at 9 P.M. returned shortly after 11 P.M. owing to high visibility.	B.N.H.
"	10-4-17	-	Quiet day. A minenwerfer Barrage was our sector to cover raid on the frontage of the Battalion on our left. Slight retaliation. Casualties 2.O.R. wounded.	P. list E. list
"	11-4-17	-	Quiet day. 12 minnies in Centre Subsector. 1.O.R. wounded.	
"	12-4-17	-	Apparent registration of Enemy on TIN BARN AVENUE, JAY POST and BOUTILLERIE Avenue working parties defined by artillery. A patrol of 3.O.R. under Lieut. Hein reconnoitred enemy lines for traces of enemy groups.	P. list

1875 Wt. W593/826 1,000,000 4/15 J.B.C. & A. A.D.S.S./Forms/C. 2118.

WAR DIARY
or
INTELLIGENCE SUMMARY

(Erase heading not required.)

Army Form C. 2118

Place	Date	Hour	Summary of Events and Information	Remarks and references to Appendices
FLEURBAIX	12-4-17	—	A Patrol 2.O.R under Lieut Cisar out to investigate enemy M.G. emplacement with intention of taking out a demolition party under that machine. Patrol observed an enemy wire to contain field.	P.T.O
"	13-4-17	—	A Patrol 3.O.R. and 2nd Lieut Grovart to locate sentry groups. Heavy minnie during night. Enemy artillery very active from 12 to 4. Patrol checked with 12 to 15 casualties. Heavy ennemi during night. Further reported by enemy. A Patrol B.O.R under Lieut Kim out to investigate enemy lines & locate sentry groups. A Patrol P.O.R. under 2nd Lieut Kilner and 15 locate sentry groups. 2 Enemy Patrols seen. Double represtable by enemy artillery, machine guns &	P.T.O
"	14-4-17	—		P.T.O
"	15-4-17	2-2.30am	Raid by enemy 35 to 40 strong, repulsed leaving 2 dead behind our casualties 1 killed 9.O.R. wounded. Quiet day afterwards. 2 Enemy Patrols seen in front subsector. 2nd Lieut. W D Grovart died of wounds.	P.T.O
"	16-4-17	—	Quiet day. Relieved by 2/5 the Kings Own (R.L R.T)	P.T.O
"	17-4-17	—	Billets resting & cleaning up equipment	P.T.O

WAR DIARY
INTELLIGENCE SUMMARY

Army Form C. 2118

Place	Date	Hour	Summary of Events and Information	Remarks and references to Appendices
FLEURBAIX	18-4-17		Billets. Working parties, training, baths.	PuR Pluk
—	19-4-17		Billets. Working parties, training, baths.	Pluk
—	20-4-17		Billets. Working parties, training, baths.	PuR
—	21-4-17		Billets. Working parties, training, baths. Army Corp. Commander granted military medal to 243435 L/Cpl Greenhalgh, 243435 Pte Arnold, and 243456 Pte J. Buckley for following circumstances:— On night 14/15 April, at 3.55 am enemy attempted a raid on N.6.1. L.G. Team, including above men, opened fire + had a stoppage. While L/C Greenhalgh cleared stoppage, rest of team fired with rifles + threw bombs. Stoppage cleared, fire from enemy wounded 5 of team including Ronalds L/C. Greenhalgh cleared stoppage, re-opened fire. Pte Buckley assisting him and Ronalds though wounded filled pans with ammunition. Enemy driven off leaving 2 dead behind and taking other casualties with them.	B B B
—	22-4-17		Billets. Working parties, training.	
—	23-4-17		do. do.	
—	24-4-17		Battalion inspected by C.O. Battalion relieved 1/5th Kings Bn (R.L) Regt. Left FLEURBAIX at 8.45 pm. Relief complete 11 pm. Night quiet. No patrols out.	
—	25-4-17		Very quiet day. A patrol of 2 other ranks under Lieut H.R. MONEY left T.31.1. and examined enemy wire 3 hard left at N.6.C. B. Braithin an enemy ditch. 2 of enemy opened fire on	

WAR DIARY
or
INTELLIGENCE SUMMARY

Army Form C. 2118

Place	Date	Hour	Summary of Events and Information	Remarks and references to Appendices
FLEURBAIX	25.4.17		in them at 40 yds distance. Two of enemy team & subsequently lost sight of. Another patrol of 4 other ranks under 2/Lieut A.R. RICKARD left at N.5.2. and reconnoitred in front of WATER FORT. No hostile patrol encountered. Enemy heard moving along withdrawn, and talking heard in TURK POINT.	&
	26.4.17		Quiet day throughout. At 11 pm 2/Lt McCLINTON & 4 O.R. crossed N.M's LAND & N.11.a.3.8. Apparently only occupation of enemy line in vicinity was a Sentry group about N.11.a.5.7. At 9.30 am 2nd Lt KILNER & 8 O.R. lay up at O.1.a.1.8 to harass patrols. Nothing seen or heard except a humming sound at O.1.a.1.6 which was dispersed by L.G.	&
	27.4.17		Another quiet day with the exception of 30 to 40 in BOUTILLERIE AVE. which were observed in trees/places. Great movement of enemy observed but nothing to cause suspicion. Box respirators were worn by enemy troops in the trenches, but not by working parties. Patrol of 2/Lieut was watching these N M's LAND, nothing seen or heard in front of N.5.2 & N.S.3 Reconnoitred - good escape in trenches. Wire improved opposite N.4.1 & N.5.1.	&

WAR DIARY or INTELLIGENCE SUMMARY

Army Form C. 2118

Place	Date	Hour	Summary of Events and Information	Remarks and references to Appendices
FLEURBAIX	28.4.17		Day fairly quiet. 10 Minnies other than T.M. in addition to Whizz Bangs &c — principally retaliation. 2nd Lt. Grew + 8 ORs left us N.6 b.6.6 and reached enemy wire at O.1.a.1.6. 2 automatic rifles + M.G. located. 2nd Lt. WOOD + 3 ORs left us N.6.4.15 but had to withdraw owing to M.G. fire. 2nd Lt. RICKARD + 4 ORs left us N.5.c.05.05 + reached N.11.a.55.95 + then N.11.a.60.85.	
	29.4.17		Quiet day. Surprise change of troops opposite. 2nd Lt. MCCLINTON + 4 ORs left N.5.d.12.70 and observed enemy wiring party about N.5.d.35.25. Patrol returned + directed L.G. fire on enemy.	
	30.4.17		Another quiet day, with exception of 35 5.9 in BREWERY. 2nd Lt. GREEN + 8 ORs left I.31.1 and accounted drink a casualty from fragment of trench mortar. New sap truck not seen. Runners prevented it close O.1.a.28.73. 4 enemy groups located within a distance of 300x of frontier. Lt. HEIN + 6 ORs left N.5.c.05.05. & reached N.11.a.15.60. While lying up, heavy trench + enemy trench mortar activity protection fire G.6. a minute. Apparent us N.11.c.35.60. On patrol eventually returned + enemy observed in h L.G. + Rifle Grenades. Lt. TIL + 4 ORs left N.6.3.1 + eventually reached N.6.c.9.6. Enemy was very much. Sixty groups located.	

Vol 4

Confidential

Diary

150th
Inf. Bn. Royal North Lancashire Regiment
From 1st May 1917 to 31st May 1917.

Volume 4.

WAR DIARY or INTELLIGENCE SUMMARY

Army Form C. 2118

(Erase heading not required.)

Place	Date	Hour	Summary of Events and Information	Remarks and references to Appendices
FLEURBAIX	1/5/17		Quiet day. LT TILL + 7 O.Rs marched N 6 c 35.50 when movement heard and two figures spotted – 1 in front + 1 in left – 25 yards away, sounds working with the intention of cutting off our patrol. Patrol retired 3 movements halted for some time to throw track. Whole party withdrew from line. Enemy lost sight of time. 2nd Lt GREEN + 4 O.Rs reached O 1 a 45.80 where patrol remained. Enemy seen fired on our patrol which then moved slightly to left when 3 enemy fired on them. Retired. Retirement necessary. 2nd Lt McCLINTON + 7 O.Rs went out and lay up at N 5 a 70.25 in wait for enemy party to repair damage done to wire in front of NECK TRENCH by our T.M. Enemy party did not turn up.	B
	2/5/17		Artillery very active both on own front line + on battery positions. Relief completed 12.30 a.m. by 1/5th King's Own (R.L.) Regt.	B
	3/5/17		BILLETS. Working parties.	B
	4/5/17		BILLETS. Working Parties. Training	B
	5/5/17		BILLETS. Working Parties. Training + Rests	B
	6/5/17		BILLETS. Working parties + Training	B
	7/5/17		BILLETS. Working parties. Training & Rests. FLEURBAIX shelled, one shell dropping near Hospital + killing 1 man. BAC ST MAUR SAILLY + ERQUINGHEM also shelled. 8.45 from Gs alarm, from 1 gun small 9pm – 11pm Green 1 active shorts in 2 min shorts in enemy back area	B

WAR DIARY / INTELLIGENCE SUMMARY

Army Form C. 2118

Place: FLEURBAIX

Date	Hour	Summary of Events and Information	Remarks and references to Appendices
8/5/17		BILLETS. Working parties training & bath. BAC ST MAUR & FLEURBAIX again shelled during day. A/c 9.30pm enemy bombardment & attempted raid on I 31.1 Battalion stood to until 10.15pm.	S.
9/5/17		BILLETS. Working parties, training & bath. BAC ST MAUR & FLEURBAIX shelled during day.	S.
10/5/17		BILLETS. Heavy shelling of Battery (R.L.) Ridge complete 11.30pm.	S.
11/5/17		Quiet day. At night our patrol examined wire at N.6.2 + N.6.3. Special patrol of 2 Officers + 5 ORs located enemy sentry group in M.11.a. 4.5.6.3 and also located gaps in enemy wire.	S.
12/5/17		Fairly quiet day. Special patrol again sent for further reconnaissance. Enemy artillery fairly active on trenches, about 100 shells falling. Suggested registration a/c 10.30pm. A raiding party consisting of O.C. Raid (Lieut. T. HOLLIS), 3 Officers + 30 other ranks operated on NED TRENCH the intention of the Assault Party was to attack the hostile sentry group in M.11.a. 4.5.6.3. hr to enemy trench. Entrance effected. Dispositions taken known. The other 2 members of the Assault Party. The last man to leave. The patrol bolted. Raiding Party & prisoner returned to our lines without any casualties. Break enforced. Approach across ground, no enemy.	S.

Army Form C. 2118

WAR DIARY
or
INTELLIGENCE SUMMARY
(Erase heading not required.)

Instructions regarding War Diaries and Intelligence Summaries are contained in F.S. Regs., Part II. and the Staff Manual respectively. Title Pages will be prepared in manuscript.

Place	Date	Hour	Summary of Events and Information	Remarks and references to Appendices
FLEURBAIX	14/5/17		Enemy Artillery registering on trenches & C.T. Otherwise nothing unusual during night.	
	15/5/17		Very quiet day and night.	
	16/5/17		Very quiet. At night a few minnies sent over.	
	17/5/17		Very quiet. Relieved by 7/5th King's Own (R.L.) Regt.	
	18/5/17		BILLETS.	
	19/5/17		do. Training. Bath & Working Parties	
	20/5/17		do	
	21/5/17		do	
	22/5/17		do	
	23/5/17		do Draft of 41 men arrived	
	24/5/17		do	
	25/5/17		do Inspection of drawing by G.O.C. Brigade.	
	26/5/17		do Inspection by G.O.C. Brigade. Relief of 7/5th King's Own (R.L.) Regt.	
	27/5/17		Very quiet day & night. At night 2/Lt GREEN + 4 O.R. left our lines and lay up outside enemy wire N 6 c 7.3. M.Gun was attempt was to enemy transport. Draft of 5 men arrived by Trench Fortress firing rifles + Very lights from various points.	
	28/5/17		Very quiet day + night. At night Lt CARRIE + 4 O.R. left our lines and lay up outside enemy wire at N 6 c 80.55. 2 Sentry groups located.	

Army Form C. 2118

WAR DIARY
or
INTELLIGENCE SUMMARY
(Erase heading not required.)

Instructions regarding War Diaries and Intelligence Summaries are contained in F.S. Regs., Part II. and the Staff Manual respectively. Title Pages will be prepared in manuscript.

Place	Date	Hour	Summary of Events and Information	Remarks and references to Appendices
FLEURBAIX	28/5/17		Afternoon very quiet they night. At night 2/Lt McCLINTON & 5 O.R's reached enemy wire at N5c.95.10. Trench apparently occupied by hostile patrol.	Q
	29/5/17		Quiet except for retaliation for our artillery. At night all quiet. Patrols were sent out for special reasons.	Q
	30/5/17		Our Artillery active all day especially on MINENWERFER when they fired in retaliation for our T.M.B. 2/Lt GREEN & 16 O.R's left at N5.b.5.15 and saw seven patrol which retired. E.F.L. MINENWERFER about N5.d.1.4.m and South group fired enemy in reputation s/w reinforcements on 28/5/17. 2/Lt RICHARDS & 5 O.R's left at N5.d.4.7 and had to return owing to illuminations on right, having reached enemy wire opposite judging by the noise of songs & talk. Lt CARRIE & 4 men acted as covering party for R.E. officer reconnoitring N.M's LAND.	Q
	31/5/17 3.30a.m		Enemy Salient raid on N6.c. & N6.3 Salient by parties of 47 men Sixty Group & upwards of 50 men in each wave & known at above Shower of trench mortars & rifle grenades. The remaining 3 men retired as soon as the alarm. Sixty Group reporting and Battle Patrol reached the scene of action almost immediately and German Officer & 3 other ranks (2 wounded) were found in trench near the SALIENT apex and surrendered without resistance.	

WAR DIARY

INTELLIGENCE SUMMARY

Place	Date	Hour	Summary of Events and Information	Remarks and references to Appendices
FLEURBAIX	31/5/15	3.30 a.m.	Enemy raided BOUTILLERIE SALIENT with party of 2 Officers & about 40 men, Sentry Group in front of SALIENT saw 12 Germans in N. Ms Land and three lines of them, and wishing to procure accidental supported heavy casualties N.C.O in charge sent back 2 men for assistance, while he & the remainder of the Group continued to harry the enemy until heavy casualties had reduced his party to himself (wounded in the knee) & one man. The N.C.O then ordered a retirement, and had to be assisted out of the bay by the remaining man. At the moment the next sentry Group arrived on the scene followed by the Battle Patrol and accepted the surrender of 1 German Officer & 3 other ranks (2 wounded). Our casualties were 2 and 6 wounded & 2 wounded. Very special [?] thanks were of the Bay, and rig he [illegible]	✓ ✓

CONFIDENTIAL.

Headquarters,
57th Division.

Herewith War Diary for the Battalion under my Command,
covering period 1/6/1917 to 30/6/1917.

R. H. Harrison, Lieut & Adjt
for Lieut-Col.,
1/7/17.   Commdg. 4/5th Bn. L. N. Lancashire Regt.

Confidential

15a

Diary

1/5th Bn. Royal North Lancashire Regiment
from 1st June 1917 to 30th June 1917.

15 June 5.

17.82

WAR DIARY
INTELLIGENCE SUMMARY
(Erase heading not required.)

Army Form C. 2118

Place	Date	Hour	Summary of Events and Information	Remarks and references to Appendices
BOUTILLERIE SUBSECTOR	1/4/17		Fairly quiet. Enemy Artillery inactive except in retaliation for our fire, occasionally quite during night	
FLEURBAIX	2/6/17		Fairly heavy Artillery fire on both Billets + Rear.	
	3/6/17		Training, Working parties + Rests.	
	4/6/17		do	Believed Lyt H. GITTINS, 1/5th K.O.(R.L.) Regt. Died of wounds. ref by Bde BM/—
	5/6/17		do	
	6/6/17		do	
	7/6/17		do	
	8/6/17		do	
	9/6/17		do	
	10/6/17		"	Relieved 1/5th K.O.(R.L.) Regt.
BOUTILLERIE Sub Sector	11/6/17		Quiet until 6 pm when enemy having shelled Support Line Patrol landed sentry group at N.10 + 9.80.3. Minnie + Pine Apple in afternoon and except for Light Minnies in enemy's Patrol made away an trenches at N.11 + 30.65. Too strong to see any, Enemy future Minnie from N.6 to 60.55 at N.6 at 80.30. Entry of E.F.L. impossible owing to our patrols minimising patrols, and found section impossible owing to our patrols being discovered.	
	12/6/17			

Army Form C. 2118

WAR DIARY
or
INTELLIGENCE SUMMARY
(Erase heading not required.)

Instructions regarding War Diaries and Intelligence Summaries are contained in F. S. Regs., Part II. and the Staff Manual respectively. Title Pages will be prepared in manuscript.

Place	Date	Hour	Summary of Events and Information	Remarks and references to Appendices
BOUTILLERIE SUB-SECTOR	13/6/17		Very quiet day and night	
	14/6/17		Very quiet day, except for light T.M. in late afternoon. Patrol one hour on beat for enemy wiring patrol. Nothing seen. Another patrol came in contact with enemy patrol about N.6.6.6.9.25. Enemy patrol retired immediately. No casualties claimed.	
	15/6/17		A day of minor & joint operations etc. Otherwise uneventful.	
	16/6/17		Very quiet except for slight retaliation with light Minnies for our L.T.M. Bde. Our patrols visited enemy wire & located enemy working party in NEAT LANE. Our Artillery dispersed enemy with casualties. Another patrol visited enemy line in NEJ TRENCH but observed enemy wiring party.	
	17/6/17		Very quiet during day. Relieved by "4th" King's Own (R.L.) Regt.	
FLEURBAIX	18/6/17		Bleu. Rest	
	19/6/17		Training. Baths & working parties	

WAR DIARY
INTELLIGENCE SUMMARY
(Erase heading not required.)

Army Form C. 2118

Place	Date	Hour	Summary of Events and Information	Remarks and references to Appendices
FLEURBAIX	20/6/17		BILLETS. Training. Working parties & Baths	
	21/6/17		" " " "	
	22/6/17		" " " "	
	23/6/17		" " " "	
	24/6/17		" " " "	
	25/6/17		Relieved 7/5th Kings Own (R.L.) Regt.	
BOUTILLERIE SUB. SECTOR	26/6/17		Fairly quiet day. At 12.3 a.m. (27/6/17) enemy raided BRIDOUX SALIENT. Heavy barrage dropped on I.31.b. N of BOUTILLERIE SALIENT, BAY AVE - HUDSON BAY POST. Left salvo group with L.G. strains from PORTUGUESE threw back party of enemy in N.M.L. about opposite left of I.31.1. Our '6' recalled & slightly wounded (1 gunshot returned to duty). The north of these parties has no experience of the enemy raid or left interruption.	✓✓✓✓✓✓
	27/6/17		Enemy Artillery very quiet throughout day & night. Enemy M.G. 18 pdrs, with new No.156 fuse, harassing at 3 places on Battalion front. he night 3 patrols etc. the supports. 2 gaps in wire entirely free except for the German dead. The enemy have unoccupied filled up the gap, not covering here, but did not prevent the patrol from entering the enemy front line. Another patrol reported the 3rd Gap in NECK TRENCH under repair with strong wiring covering party in front. 18 pdrs harassed the working party not afterwards been dispersed when they attempted to resume work. 3rd Patrol entered IVES TRENCH	✓

Army Form C. 2118

WAR DIARY
INTELLIGENCE SUMMARY
(Erase heading not required.)

Instructions regarding War Diaries and Intelligence Summaries are contained in F.S. Regs., Part II. and the Staff Manual respectively. Title Pages will be prepared in manuscript.

Place	Date	Hour	Summary of Events and Information	Remarks and references to Appendices
BOUTILLERIE SUB-SECTOR	27/6/17		Enemy much the same as recent. Enemy snipers' loopholes, and also 2 M.G.s	
	28/6/17		Enemy Trench Mortars active, principally in retaliation for our T.M. shoots. During night, enemy attempting to strengthen his wire in NEAR by throwing out knife rests to own parapet. The parties carrying his attempts to wire were soon stopped by L.G. Another patrol examined wire in front of NEAT & NEBULA and found no unpassable. Another patrol examined wire in front of WATER FORT (NECK), and found it in fairly good condition.	
	29/6/17		Quiet day until 3 pm when Battalion on left raided at BRIDOUX FORT. The enemy barrages on front line & CTs on top line in TIM BARRY AVENUE, and adjacent to the raid - an top line in TIM BARRY AVENUE. On patrol at night examined wire in front of NECK and another Enemier in front of NEBULA. Work interrupted by enemy minenwerfer which opened heavily then recommenced. Our patrol withdrawing Artillery on our trenches, and own Artillery replying, then recommenced.	
	30/6/17		Enemy very unsettled to-day. Repeatedly using his Artillery in short bursts on own trenches.	

Confidential.

War   Diary

of

4th Bn. Royal East Lancashire Regiment.
From 1st July 1917 to 31st July 1917.

Volume 6.

WAR DIARY or INTELLIGENCE SUMMARY

Army Form C. 2118

(Erase heading not required.)

Instructions regarding War Diaries and Intelligence Summaries are contained in F.S. Regs., Part II. and the Staff Manual respectively. Title Pages will be prepared in manuscript.

Place	Date	Hour	Summary of Events and Information	Remarks and references to Appendices
FLEURBAIX	1/7/17		BILLETS. Rest. "B" Company to old Reinforcement Camp for Special training.	✓
	2/7/17		" Training, Baths & Working parties.	✓
	3/7/17		" "	✓
	4/7/17		" "	✓
	5/7/17		" "	✓
	6/7/17		Inspection by G.O.C. Brigade. "B" Company returned from old Reinforcement Camp. Relief of 1/5th K.O. (R.L.) Regt.	✓
BOUTILLERIE SUB-SECTOR	7/7/17	9.20 pm	Enemy placed heavy barrage on our trenches from N.5 to T.31.1. Attempted raid suspected on RUE du BOIS SECTOR on left, in rain but been anticipated then for several days. Enemy continued until 12 midnight.	✓
	8/7/17		Very quiet day except for retaliation for own T.M's.	✓
	9/7/17		Quiet day. Own T.M's to Mining ridge.	✓
	10/7/17		Our T.M's very heavy than retaliation. During night enemy patrol in N.M. Land driven back.	✓
	11/7/17		T.M's again heavy with heavy retaliation. Enemy inactive except in retaliation. Enemy wiring parties out during night.	✓

Army Form C. 2118

WAR DIARY
or
INTELLIGENCE SUMMARY

(Erase heading not required.)

Instructions regarding War Diaries and Intelligence Summaries are contained in F. S. Regs., Part II. and the Staff Manual respectively. Title Pages will be prepared in manuscript.

Place	Date	Hour	Summary of Events and Information	Remarks and references to Appendices
BOUTILLERIE SUB-SECTOR	12.7.17		Enemy very active with their T.M. Considerable damage done. One of our patrols (9 men) was attacked by enemy fighting patrol of about 40 men & flank parties of 15 + a frontal party of 10. On patrol returning along wire and when enemy about 10 yards away opened rapid fire. Enemy waited for this over lines, some of them apparently casualties, being helped back. Our patrol too small to follow up their success.	
	13.7.17		Fired little except in retaliation. Enemy active. Saw estimated strength 8-10 men. Driven off by rifle fire & bombs. Aeroplane squadron of 10-15 planes over lines during night.	
	14.7.17		Surprise registration of our C.T.s + part of Braun's Line by enemy at night from "B.C." in the form of 7 fighting patrols in a frontage of about 1200 yards. Army to strain darkness we were in ignorance of formation rain - helped them the other attacks in finding gap in enemy line. Enemy from the company opposite the fighting patrols all were returned at dawn without leaving any identification casualties, and without any identification.	
	15.7.17		Very Quiet day. Relieved by 1/5th K.O. (R.L.) Regt.	

1875 Wt. W593/826 1,000,000 4/15 I.B.C. & A. A.D.S.S./Forms/C. 2118.

WAR DIARY or INTELLIGENCE SUMMARY

Army Form C. 2118

Place	Date	Hour	Summary of Events and Information	Remarks and references to Appendices
FLEURBAIX	16/7/17		BILLETS. REST.	
	17/7/17		Training, Baths & Working Parties. "B" Co. Special training for Raid	
	18/7/17		" " " "	
	19/7/17		" " " "	
	20/7/17		"B" Company carried out in the form of a fighting patrol - 1312 Strength 4 Officers & 130 O.R. - in N.E.D., NECK & NEBULA TRENCHES in enemy outpost line front to CORDONNERIE SECTOR. Our Artillery was opened to encourage Frags but the fire of the bombardment increased from M.G. fire preventing difficulties of working parties. Our patrols returned to own trenches at 3 a.m. with 7 casualties - only two being wounded.	
	21/7/17		Training, Baths & working parties	
	22/7/17		REST. Relief of 7/5 K.O.(R.L.) Regt.	
BOUTILLERIE SUB-SECTOR	23/7/17		Bn. at 10.30 pm 5 Scouts dropped in neighbourhood of TIN BARN TRAMLINE. Nor a most front. Nothing of interest happened. At night 3 patrols sent up fighting Patrol located 7 parties of enemy in E.F.L. but apparently not performing to conctement.	
	24/7/17		Very quiet except for retaliation to our L.T. Mr. Night very quiet. 3 Patrols out but nothing of interest occurred.	

WAR DIARY or INTELLIGENCE SUMMARY

Army Form C. 2118

(Erase heading not required.)

Instructions regarding War Diaries and Intelligence Summaries are contained in F.S. Regs., Part II. and the Staff Manual respectively. Title Pages will be prepared in manuscript.

Place	Date	Hour	Summary of Events and Information	Remarks and references to Appendices
BOUTILLERIE SUB-SECTOR	25/7/17		Very quiet day. At night 2 patrols out. One met 2 enemy patrols apparently lying in wait for it. Retired without encounter.	
	26/7/17		Fairly quiet. The Right Subsector had about 40 5.9, 4.2 + 77— at night. One patrol was almost enveloped by Sonnenblume formation of enemy in No Man's Land. The enemy patrols appeared rather in decoy.	
	27/7/17		Quiet in trenches, but heavy gun firing made the whole day on FLEURBAIX. At night 3 patrols out.	
	28/7/17		Very quiet day. At night 3 patrols out. 2 enemy patrols seen but no encounter.	
	29/7/17		Again a very quiet day. Quiet day, except for retaliation to our T.M. shoot. During the night parties were carried out in NED TRENCH + NEAT TRENCH, also something that in the afternoon being at intervals + shell broken ground. The NED trench only partially shown so + later on N.E.F. No sign of occupation. 2 formed defences. The enemy appeared to be inactive. The avenue to the NEAT trench which was fired on with rifle + trench mortar ammunition by enemy. E.F.L. fired. We did not suffer any casualties.	
	30/7/17			

Army Form C. 2118

WAR DIARY
or
INTELLIGENCE SUMMARY
(Erase heading not required.)

Place	Date	Hour	Summary of Events and Information	Remarks and references to Appendices
POUTILLERIE SUB-SECTOR	31/7/17		Low visibility. Very quiet day & night. During the night she[?] be retaliation for operations by Batt. on our left. No hostile air.	8.

Confidential

Headquarters
39th Division

Eleventh War Diary of
the Battalion under my
Command covering period 1st
to 31st August 1917.

Calyd Harford
1917   Comndg. H? L L R Regt. Lt-Col

Confidential.

War Diary

4th. Battalion Royal North Lancashire Regiment
From 1st. August 1917 to 31st. August 1917.

Volume 7.

Army Form C. 2118

WAR DIARY
INTELLIGENCE SUMMARY
(Erase heading not required.)

Instructions regarding War Diaries and Intelligence Summaries are contained in F.S. Regs., Part II. and the Staff Manual respectively. Title Pages will be prepared in manuscript.

Place	Date	Hour	Summary of Events and Information	Remarks and references to Appendices
FAUQUI ART BOUTILLERIE SUB-SECTOR	1/8/17		Quiet day in Trenches. Relieved at night by the 1st LEICESTERSHIRE REGT	
FLEURBAIX	2/8/17		Billets. At night marched to ARMENTIERES.	
ARMENTIERES	3/8/17		do. Preparation of cellar billets. Clearing of Emergency Routes, etc. during night. Enemy heavily shelled ARMENTIERES.	
	4/8/17		do. Clearing Emergency Routes and Shelter huts. Quiet night.	
	5/8/17		do. do.	
	6/8/17		do. do.	
	7/8/17		do. do.	
	8/8/17		do. do.	
	9/8/17		do. do. Relief of 1 Ys K.O.(R.)Regt.	
HOUPLINES	10/8/17	4.30	Enemy attempted small raid by about 10 men. On Enemy (wounded) taken prisoner. Subsequently died in hut so reasonable. During day enemy shelling trenches normal. At night E.pair on Batt on night. E. bombs from 8.pm to 9 p.m. on right half of our sector. Otherwise quiet night.	
	11/8/17		Normal activity of E. artillery fire. During night patrol reconnoitring N.M.Lans.	
	12/8/17		Normal activity of E. artillery fire. At night patrol reconnuting.	

WAR DIARY
INTELLIGENCE SUMMARY
(Erase heading not required.)

Army Form C. 2118

Place	Date	Hour	Summary of Events and Information	Remarks and references to Appendices
HOUTLINES	12/9/17		Normal day. Gas rocket being shelled by ARMENTIERES. 3 patrols a/c night reconnaissance N.M.L.	
	13/9/17		Enemy shells found on our line at 2.30 p.m. Enemy which normal. During night 3 patrols sent out. Patrol of 12 men reached the enemy ditch and were seen by the enemy in the retirement one man was wounded & had to be carried back to our line by 2nd Lt BELL & Capt FORSHAW, but two men were missing. One of the wounded men returned at own late.	&
	15/9/17		Fairly quiet day. Enemy active during night. Rate 10.5 cm + 7.7 cm Patrols reconnoitred N.M.L.	&
	16/9/17		Enemy artillery active in the left of Sector. 2 patrols at night reconnoitred N.M.L.	&
	17/9/17		Quiet day. Two companies relieved by two companies of the 7/5th K.O. (R.L.) Regt.	&
	18/9/17		Relief by 7/5 K.O. (R.L.) Regt. completed.	&
ARMENTIERES	19/9/17		Billets	&
	20/9/17		Training Batln + Working parties	&
	21/9/17		" " "	&
	22/9/17		" " "	&

Army Form C. 2118

WAR DIARY
or
INTELLIGENCE SUMMARY
(Erase heading not required.)

Instructions regarding War Diaries and Intelligence Summaries are contained in F. S. Regs., Part II. and the Staff Manual respectively. Title Pages will be prepared in manuscript.

Place	Date	Hour	Summary of Events and Information	Remarks and references to Appendices
ARMENTIÈRES	23/8/17		Billets - Training, Baths & Working Parties	8
	24/8/17		"	8
	25/8/17		"	8
	26/8/17		"	8
		9.30 am	Steady shelling of H.Q. billet. No direct hits.	
			Relieved 7.K.O.I. (R.A.) Reg.t	
HOUPLINES	27/8/17		Fairly quiet day & night.	8
	28/8/17		Exceptional movement in E. line from 6.45 am to 9.30 am. Railway Sapette. E. artillery active with 4.2- during day. Very quiet during night.	8
	29/8/17		E. artillery fairly active on Left Company Sector. Quiet at night.	8
	30/8/17		Enemy artillery fairly quiet. Own patrols active at night.	8
	31/8/17		Artillery action on our Frenchs during day. Exceptionally quiet during night.	8

Headquarters
66th Division

Herewith War Diary of
the Unit under my command,
period 1/9/17 to 30/9/17.

2/10/17.

Ashley L. Barford.
Lieut. Colonel,
Comdg. 4/5 Loyal North Lanc. Regt.

Vol 8

Confidential

War
Diary
of
1/5th Battalion Loyal North Lancashire Regiment
From 1st September 1917 to 30th September 1917.

Volume 6.

WAR DIARY or INTELLIGENCE SUMMARY

Army Form C. 2118.

(Erase heading not required.)

Instructions regarding War Diaries and Intelligence Summaries are contained in F. S. Regs., Part II. and the Staff Manual respectively. Title pages will be prepared in manuscript.

Place	Date	Hour	Summary of Events and Information	Remarks and references to Appendices
HOUPLINES	1.9.17	10 a.m.	Heavy bombardment of Lumerous 80+ km No.7 Post & Rifle grenades fired at No.6 No. 4 mortar engine Germany trapped. Retaliatory Brit. Normal Artillery & T.M.	
-do-	2.9.17	2 a.m.	30-40 enemy came over and wire in No. 9. Driven off by rifle fire, lys. fighter, lights, Normal Artillery & T.M. fire. Total enemy hand grenade fire.	
-do-	3.9.17		Relieved by 2/5 Bn. KOR Lanc. Regt. Marched to Billets in ARMENTIÈRES.	
ARMENTIÈRES	4.9.17		Billets - Baths, training &c. Shelling of battery in Park. No casualties.	
-do-	5.9.17		Billets - Baths, training &c.	
-do-	6.9.17		Billets - Baths, training &c.	
-do-	7.9.17		Billets - Baths, training &c.	
-do-	8.9.17		Billets - Baths, training &c.	
-do-	9.9.17		Billets - Baths, training &c.	
-do-	10.9.17		Billets - Baths, training &c.	
-do-	11.9.17		Relief of 2/5 B. KOR Lanc Regt.	
HOUPLINES	12.9.17	4.5 a.m.	Enemy Light Howitzer opened fire on No. 5 Post. Gassed not attained.	
-do-	-do-		Normal Artillery & T.M. fire. Aircraft active - stray bombs. Part of bombs whistle fired into Ball. all quiet.	
-do-	-do-		2 Gas bombardments at 8.15 p.m. & 2 a.m. by T.M. Men mainly gassed. 13 gassed to casualty clearing station.	
-do-	13.9.17	8.30 a.m.	Enemy put down heavy barrage of artillery & T.M's including smoke shells in loc 14-15-16-17. F.S Signal sipping for alarm	
			sent out our artillery fired SOS at 8.40 a.m. Enemy plan were apparently to commit raid of No.7 Post. but	

A6945 Wt. W11422/M1160 350,000 12/16 D. D. & L. Forms/C/2118/14.

Army Form C. 2118.

WAR DIARY
INTELLIGENCE SUMMARY.
(Erase heading not required.)

Place	Date	Hour	Summary of Events and Information	Remarks and references to Appendices
HOUPLINES	12.9.17	8.3-	Infantry attack repulsed. Our doubt [enemy] to promptly effective reply by our artillery. Fine days on No 7 Post demolished & FK pit L/1/9 Post to L/3/6 No 7 Post rendered unapproachable temporally by shell	
-do-	"		In many places. Our casualties 1 OR Killed 1 OR Wounded. Casualty inflicted [illegible] enemy unknown	
-do-	"		of day on Left Coy sector. During night 500-600 footballs in turns / 15 lieutenants on Right Coy sector.	
-do-	14.9.17		Normal day. 3.30 p.m 10 a.m shelling of Post 13 with 4.2's and minenwerfer. No damage. Very quiet night.	
-do-	15.9.17		Quiet day & night.	
-do-	16.9.17		Enemy artillery active in morning. Quiet for rest of day. At night	
			relieved by the 2nd West Reg. and proceeded to camp at	
			WATERLANDS. (36 N.W. B.20 d.9.4.)	
WATERLANDS	17.9.17		In REST.	
	18.9.17		March to NEUF BERQUIN. (S.A-L.14)	
NEUF BERQUIN	19.9.17		- LA PIERRIÈRE (36 A P 14.d.0) V. ROBECQ + BUSNES	
LA PIERRIÈRE	20.9.17		" RELY (36A-T.1) " LILLERS, FAUQUEMBERGH & LIÈTRES	
RELY	21.9.17		REST.	
	22.9.17		Cleaning up	
	23.9.17			

WAR DIARY
INTELLIGENCE SUMMARY
(Erase heading not required.)

Army Form C. 2118.

Place	Date	Hour	Summary of Events and Information	Remarks and references to Appendices
RELY	24/9/17		REST	
"	25/9/17		TRAINING	
"	26/9/17		"	
"	27/9/17		"	
"	28/9/17		"	
"	29/9/17		Sunday	
"	30/9/17		"	

Confidential

No. 9

War

Acts. Battalion Royal North Lancashire Regiment
from 1st October 1916 to 31st October 1917.

Volume 9

WAR DIARY
INTELLIGENCE SUMMARY
(Erase heading not required.)

Army Form C. 2118.

Instructions regarding War Diaries and Intelligence Summaries are contained in F. S. Regs., Part II. and the Staff Manual respectively. Title pages will be prepared in manuscript.

Place	Date	Hour	Summary of Events and Information	Remarks and references to Appendices
RELY	1/10/17		REST BILLETS Training &c	
	2/10/17		do	
	3/10/17		do	
	4/10/17		do	
	5/10/17		do	
	6/10/17		Inspection by G.O.C. General Turner during the Inst Pm urge special attention paid to attention to the attack position the telling of object points & look-out	
	7/10/17		do (Sunday) Training	
	8/10/17		(Monday) Rest	
	9/10/17		Training	
	10/10/17		do	
	11/10/17		do	
	12/10/17		do	
	13/10/17		do	
	14/10/17		do	
	15/10/17		do Brigade Sports	
	16/10/17		do	

WAR DIARY
or
INTELLIGENCE SUMMARY.
(Erase heading not required.)

Army Form C. 2118.

Place	Date	Hour	Summary of Events and Information	Remarks and references to Appendices
CAMPAGNE	17.10.17		Marched from RELY	
PROVEN	18.10.17		From CAMPAGNE to PROVEN in Buy Quartered in PADDINGTON CAMP	
	19.10.17		At PROVEN Resting	
	20.10.17		" Training + Cleaning up	
	21.10.17		" Sunday Church Parade	
	22.10.17		" Training	
	23.10.17		Moved to BOESINGHE & Marched to Bivouac Ground	
	24.10.17		During day carried extra ration, water & ammunition to dump at 4 pm marched by Track "A" to relieve the 10th Lincolns (101st By Brigade) - V.16 good. V.16 boys Relief completed about 11.30 pm	
Front line	25.10.17		From line at Shell Crater - Occupies line all day. Normal shelling. Nothing of interest	
	26.10.17		Attack launched at 5 Ho am Bugles Horns + Coys of Rifleson & attacked	
	27.10.17		Released at 5.30 am by Company of 1st Kings and marched to MUDDLESTONE CAMP where hot meal served. Entrained at BOESINGHE at 11.30 AM & trained at PROVEN & proceeded to No.1. Area Camp	

WAR DIARY
INTELLIGENCE SUMMARY.
(Erase heading not required.)

Army Form C. 2118.

Place	Date	Hour	Summary of Events and Information	Remarks and references to Appendices
PROVEN	28/10/17		In Camp. Testing Refitting &	
"	29/10/17		" " "	
"	30/10/17		" " "	
"	31/10/17		Training &	

170TH INF. BDE. ORDER NO. 82.

Ref: Maps. 1/10,000. SCHAAP BALIE.
BROEMBEEK.
ST JULIEN.

---

1. On O day at an hour (Zero) to be notified later the 57th Division will carry out an attack in conjunction with the 173rd Inf. Bde., 58th Division, on the right, and 149th Inf. Bde., 50th Div. on the left.

2. The attack on the 57th Div. front will be carried out by the 170th Inf. Bde. A battalion of the 171st Inf. Bde. will be placed at the disposal of the G.O.C. 170th Inf. Bde. for use in case of emergency.

Allotment of troops. 3. The attack will be carried out by the 2/5th L.N.L.Regt. on the right, 2/4th L.N.L. Regt. in the centre and 4/5th L.N.L.R. on the left, with 2/5th King's Own Regt. (less 1 Coy.) in support, and a Bn. of the 171st Inf. Bde. in Reserve.

Objectives. 4. The final objective of the 170th Inf. Bde. will be:-
 (i) A line V.15.a.00.75 - V.8.d.55.60 - V.2.c.5.1.
 (ii) A line V.14.b.98.72 - V.8.b.9.3 - V.2.d.6.0 - V.2.d.10.55.
The final objective will be consolidated as laid down in Bde. Preliminary Instructions No. 5.

Dividing Lines. 5. As laid down in para. 4 170th Inf. Bde. Instructions No. 5.

Method of Attack. 6. This will be as laid down in para. 5 170th Inf. Bde. Instructions No. 5.

Forming up 7. As soon as the position of the initial barrage is communicated to Bn. Comdrs. they will arrange to tape out their forming up lines 200 yds. behind the barrage line.
All troops will be formed up on the forming up line by Zero minus two hours, at which time all troops in front of the forming up line will withdraw.
As soon as the barrage comes down at Zero hour the troops will move forward till the 1st wave is within 50-75 of the barrage, before it lifts.
2/5th King's Own Regt. will be formed on the approximate line LANDING FM: - WATER HOUSE by zero minus one hour.
The Battalion, 171st Inf. Bde. will be formed up in EAGLE TRENCH ready to move forward at zero hour if so ordered.

Barrage. 8. Full details of the Barrage have not yet been received.
 (a) The first lift will be at Zero plus 8 mins.
 (b) The barrage will move forward at the rate of 100 yds. in 8 mins., in 50 yd. lifts.
 (c) A protective barrage will be placed in front of the first objective, and will become intense at Zero plus 1 hour 48 mins. It will begin to move forward again at Zero plus 1 hour and 56 mins.

Action of M.Gs...... 9

Action of M.Gs.

9. 8 guns of 170th M.G. Coy. in conjunction with 8 guns of the 171st M.G. Coy. and 12 guns 173rd M.G. Coy. under the command of the D.M.G.O. will form a creeping barrage, moving 400 yds. EAST of the artillery creeping barrage.

The M.G. protective barrage will be placed 500 yds. E. of the final objective.

The 170th M.G. Coy. less 8 guns will act as laid down in para. 12, 170th Inf. Bde. Preliminary Instructions No. 5.

A.A., Lewis & M.Gs.

10. O.C. 170th M.G. Coy will arrange to place two of his guns in positions about a line V.13.d.8.8 - V.13.b.3.7 for use against low flying enemy aeroplanes.

Nos. 1, 2 and 3 of the team will accompany each gun. Remainder of teams to be kept under cover in the most convenient place within view of the gun.

14 Belt Boxes will be kept with each gun and 4000 rds. S.A.A. with the two guns.

O.C. 2/5th King's Own Regt. will detail 2 L.Gs. for A.A. work. Positions about the line U.24.b.8.4 - U.18.d.3.0. Each gun will have with it 20 drums and 2000 rds. S.A.A. Action of personnel as for A.A. M.Gs.

In the event of an advance the above Lewis and M.Gs. will conform with the movements of the Infantry.

Action of Counter Attack Bn.

11. 2/5th King's Own Regt. will act as laid down in para. 11 of Bde. Instructions No. 5.

Co-operation with Bns. of Bdes. on flanks.

12. O.C. 2/5th L.N.L. Regt. will detail a special party to obtain touch with a similar party of 173rd Inf. Bde. at SPIDER CROSS ROADS.

O.C. 4/5th L.N.L.R. will detail special parties to obtain touch with similar parties of 149th Inf. Bde. at the following points:-
Pill Box at V.8.a.05.85.
  do   at V.2.c.40.06.
Bridge at V.2.d.10.65.

Tactical Points.

13. Tactical points in the final objective are laid down in para. 5 of Bde. Instructions No. 7. These points will be tenaciously defended.

Action of L.T.Ms.

14. The 170th L.T.M.Bty. will not go into action with their guns. The battery will bivouac at C.13.d.0.3, where their guns and stores will be dumped.

Contact Aeroplanes.

15. (a) A Contact aeroplane will fly over the 57th Divnl. Front at:-
Zero plus 1 hour 30 mins.
Zero plus 2 hrs. 30 mins.
and subsequently as ordered by Corps H.Q.

Leading troops will light flares only when demanded from the aeroplane.
(a) By Klaxon Horn Signal.
(b) By a series of white lights.

No flares will be lit till called for. Flares will be lit as far as possible in bunches of 3. The importance of lighting flares and of waving to the contact aeroplane if flares are not available will be impressed on all ranks. RED flares will be used.

(b) A counter attack aeroplane will be up during daylight from Zero hour onwards.

Whenever this machine observes hostile parties of 100 or over moving to counter attack it will drop a Smoke Bomb over that portion of the
front/

front towards which the enemy is moving.

The Smoke Bomb will burst at a distance of about 100 ft. below the aeroplane, into a white parachute flare which descends slowly leaving a trail of brown smoke about one foot broad behind it.

Carrying Parties.
16. A Coy. of 2/5th King's Own Regt. and 170th L.T. M.Bty. will form the Bde. Carrying Party and will bivouac C.13.d.0.3 whence they will work under instructions from the Bde. Bombing Officer.

Headquarters.
17. At Zero hour H.Q. will be as follows:-
Adv. Bde. H.Q. — STRAY FARM.
Rear -do- — FUSILIER HOUSE, C.13.c.0.0
2/5th L.N.L.Regt. — FARDAN HOUSE.
2/4th L.N.L.Regt. — LOUIS FARM.
4/5th L.N.L.Regt. — OLGA HOUSES.
2/5th King's Own Regt. — DOUBLE COTTS.
170th M.G.Coy. — LOUIS FARM.
170th L.T.M.Bty. — C.13.d.0.3.
A Bn. 171st Inf. Bde. — DOUBLE COTTS.

O.C. 2/5th King's Own will establish H.Q. at FARDAN HOUSE on his Bn. moving forward by zero minus 1 hour.

O.C. 170th M.G.Coy. will move his H.Q. forward after Zero hour as the situation demands.

The G.O.C. 170th Inf. Bde., Bde. Major and Bde. Signalling Officer will be at Adv. Bde. H.Q.

The Staff Captain will be at Rear Bde. H.Q.

Synchronisation of Watches.
18. All Units of the Bde. will send an Officer to Adv. Bde. H.Q. STRAY FARM at 4 p.m. on the day previous to 0 day to synchronise watches.

The Bde. Intelligence Officer will be responsible for the synchronisation.

Officers attending will each carry two watches.

Seconds in Command.
19. Seconds in Command of Bns. will withdraw to rear Bde. H.Q. by zero hour on 0 day.

Signal Communications.
20. Signal arrangements are laid down in Appendix "A".

Prisoners.
21. Arrangements for collection and escorting of Prisoners are laid down in Appendix "B". With reference to para. 3 Bns. will detail two men each to collect documents, etc.

22. Barrage Map for these Operations attached.
23. ACKNOWLEDGE.

Captain,
Brigade Major,
170th Infantry Brigade.

Issued at p.m.24/10/17.

Copies to:-
1. 57th Div.(G)
2. 57th Div.(q).
3. 171st Bde.
4. 172nd Inf.Bde.
5. D.M.G.O.,57th Div.
6. 2/5th King's Own.
7. 2/4th L.N.L.
8. 2/5th L.N.L.
9. 4/5th L.N.L.
10. 170th M.G.Coy.
11. 170th L.T.M.B.
12. No. 2 Coy.Div.Tr.
13.14. 103rd Inf.Bde.
15. 58th Div.
16. 50th Div.
17. 149th Bde.
18. 173rd Bde.
19. C.R.E.,57th Div.
20. A.D.M.S.,57th Div.
21. Brigadier.
22. Bde. Major.
23. Staff Capt.
24. Bde.Bombg.Offr.
25. Bde.Trpc.Offr.
26.27. War Diary.
28.29. do.
30. Bde. I.O.
31. Bde.Sigs.170th.

APPENDIX "A".

SIGNALLING COMMUNICATIONS.

The following will be the arrangements for the operations detailed in 170th Inf. Bde. Order No. 82.

1. TELEPHONE COMMUNICATION.

From Divnl. Adv. H.Q. (C.19.c.0.9) to:-
170th Inf. Bde. in line. STRAY FARM, C.3.c.2.7 - 2 circuits.

2. WIRELESS. A Trench Wireless Set will be installed at AU BON GITE working in conjunction with Corps Directing Station at BOESINGHE CHATEAU. The latter will be in telephonic communication with Divnl. Adv. H.Q.

Messages by Wireless will be sent in "Field" Cypher.

Wireless Operators at AU BON GITE will encode or decode. At Divnl. Adv. H.Q. an Officer is attached for this purpose.

3. AMPLIFIER AND POWER BUZZER.

An Amplifier will be installed at U.23.d.4.0 to work in conjunction with Power Buzzers, one of which will be installed at the H.Q. of each of the three attacking Bns.

B.A.B. Code will be used, the message being encoded and decoded by the addressor and addressee respectively. In cases of extreme urgency, after zero hour, messages may be sent in clear, but must be be franked "By Power Buzzer in Clear", and signed by an Officer, who will be held responsible.

Bde. Signal Officer will allot time and intervals for sending, to prevent jamming.

Messages from DOUBLE COTTS to STRAY FM: (Bde.H.Q.) will be sent by telephone, runner, or visual, under Bde. arrangements.

4. VISUAL STATIONS WILL BE ESTABLISHED AS FOLLOWS:-

STRAY FARM (C.3.c.2.7)	Found by Division.
to	
THE INGS (C.4.a.3.9)	Found by Division.
to	
AU BON GITE (U.28.d.2.9) Bde. H.Q.	Found by Division.
to	
BIRD HOUSE (U.29.a.9.4)	Found by Brigade.
to	
Near DOUBLE COTTS (U.23.d.4.0)	Found by Brigade.
to	
19 METRE HILL (V.18.d.4.3).	Found by Brigade.

The latter will also act as a Central Visual Station for picking up messages from Bns. in line.

5. RUNNER SERVICE.

There are four Runners at STRAY FARM (C.3.c.2.7) and at AU BON GITE (U.28.d.1.9) to work between these two places.

A Central Runner Route forward of AU BON GITE, including Relay Posts at BIRD HOUSE, DOUBLE COTTS (U.23.d.2.2), 19 METRE HILL (V.18.d.4.3). has been arranged.

Lamps shewing a green light will be shewn at each Runner Relay Post by night.

Six of these lamps will be issued to attacking Bde., and a further limited supply can be obtained if required.

6. PIGEONS........

6. **PIGEONS.** Will be delivered to Bde. H.Q. on the afternoon and evening previous to attack on the following scale:-

    Bde. H.Q.   4 Birds.
    Bde. Forward Station (19 METRE
                             HILL)   6 Birds.
    Each Attacking Battalion.   12 Birds.
    Support Battalion.   6 Birds.
    Battalion of 171st Inf.Bde.
                attached   6 Birds.
                     Total - 58 Birds.

At least two Birds should be kept at the H.Q. of each attacking Battalion.

Messages will be sent by Pigeons when the objective is reached, a proportion of Birds being kept for further messages during the day.

All Birds which have not been used to carry messages, will be released before dusk, by which time fresh Birds will be on their way up to Bns. for use next day.

7. **BRIGADE - BATTALION TELEPHONE ETC. LINES.**

Owing to the length of lines to be maintained, it will probably be only possible to maintain one circuit from attacking Bde. H.Q. to each of its Bns.

EVERY EFFORT will be concentrated on keeping these circuits through.

8. Bde. and Battn. H.Q. will be marked by ground sheets of authorised shape with the code letter of the Unit laid out in white strips alongside. These letters will be 9 ft. in depth.

Signalling to aeroplanes will be done by panels.

9. The following are the Code Names and Calls of Bdes. on the right and left:-

Unit.	Code Call.	Code Name.
149TH INF.BDE.		
1/4th North'd Fus.	SEZ	SEIZE.
1/5th -do-	SER	SEARCH
1/6th -do-	SED	SEED.
1/7th -do-	SEC	SECT
149th M.G.Coy.	SEB	SETTER
149th T.M.Bty.	SEM	SEER
	SET	SURGE
173rd INF. BDE.		
2/1st London Regt.	UPZ	UPHILL
2/2nd -do-	UPA	UPLIFT
2/3rd -do-	UPB	UPSTART
2/4th -do-	UPP	UPPER
214th M.G.Coy.	UPS	UPSHOT.
173rd T.M.Bty.	UPM	UPSET.
	UPT	UPROAR.

APPENDIX "B".

DISPOSAL OF PRISONERS DURING OPERATIONS.

The following instructions regarding the disposal of Prisoners will be observed during the operations.

1. All Prisoners taken will be sent, under escort, by the quickest route to the Divisional Collecting Station at STRAY FARM (C.3.c.20.75) where they will be handed over to the Officer in charge and a receipt obtained for them.

Prisoners will then be sent under orders of the Officer in charge Divnl. Collecting Station direct to the advanced Corps Cage at CACTUS CORNER (B.12.d.2.4) where they will be handed over to an Officer of the Provost Staff XIV Corps and a receipt obtained for them.

2. ### EXAMINATION OF PRISONERS.

The only person with authority to examine prisoners previous to their arrival at the Corps Cage is the Divnl. Intelligence Officer and he will only ask questions of urgent tactical importance. No other questions will be put to prisoners until they arrive at the Corps Cage.

3. ### DOCUMENTS.

(a) Officers will be searched immediately they are captured and all documents, maps, &c. which may be found in their possession will be taken from them, put in a Sandbag, labelled and taken down to the Divnl. Collecting Station by the escort.

(b) Other prisoners will not be searched until they reach the Corps Cage, but escorts must be on their guard to prevent any attempt on the part of the prisoners to destroy documents, &c. on their way down to the Cage.

(c) All ranks must be warned against taking pocket books containing documents, letters, post cards &c. from prisoners and retaining them as souvenirs.

4. ### SEARCHING THE BATTLEFIELD.

(a) Each Bde. in the line will detail six men to collect documents, &c. from the Battlefield, from the enemy dead, from dugouts, Headquarters, Telephone Centres, &c.

(b) All documents found will be tied in bundles and labelled shewing where they were found.

5. ### ESCORTS.

(a) Regimental Escorts will accompany prisoners to the Divnl. Collecting Station where they will hand the prisoners over to the Officer in charge and obtain a receipt from him, after which they will at once rejoin their Unit.

(b) The proportion of escorts to prisoners will be:-
   1 man for 5 prisoners.
   2 men for 10 prisoners.

Over 10 prisoners an additional escort of 1 man to every 10 prisoners.

Where possible slightly wounded men should be used as escorts.

6. Bns. will inform Bde. H.Q. the number of prisoners captured by them at the end of a day's fighting.

REPORT UPON ATTACK MADE BY
THE 1/5TH BN. LOYAL NORTH LANCASHIRE REGT.
ON THE 26/10/17.

At 4-30 a.m. on the 26/10/17 the Battalion was drawn up on the forming up line ready to move forward.

At 5-40 a.m., zero hour, our barrage fell and the Battalion moved forward with the leading wave from 25 to 30 yards behind the barrage.

At 5-45 a.m. a light enemy barrage dropped just behind our original front line and the Company in reserve had to pass through this barrage, suffering a few casualties in so doing. The enemy barrage continued on or about this line until about 7-45 a.m. Despite the mud and waterlogged shell craters the line advanced steadily behind our own barrage and under slight enemy Machine Gun fire until about 6 a.m. and at about 6-30 a.m. the troops were finally held up on the line coloured GREEN on the attached map, a barrier of Machine Gun fire being opened up by the Machine Guns in the pillboxes immediately in front and on the flanks of our troops.

A party of men succeeded in working round a pillbox in the ruins of a farm building at V.2.a.85.30. This strongpoint held 30 men, who were killed or wounded by Lewis Gun and Rifle fire and bombs.

Two aeroplanes carried out aeroplane contact work throughout the day but few flares were lit on account of the consequent smoke giving away our new position to the enemy.

Enemy aircraft to the number of 14 machines repeatedly flew over our troops at a low altitude and inflicted several casualties.

Enemy artillery - apparently resultant upon aeroplane reconnaissance - opened fire on our new line but fortunately the shells fell about 100 yards beyond our men, and this fire was kept up most of the day. Artillery fire at intervals throughout the day swept Track A.

From 6-30 a.m. the troops with the exception of Lewis Gunners and Snipers were compelled to lie low in waterlogged shell holes owing to the sweeping Machine Gun fire and constant sniping from men posted in trees, shellcraters and pillboxes.

At 7-20 a.m. about 100 men appeared from the vicinity of DAVOUST FARM with the object apparently of delivering a counter-attack. The men were totally disorganised and in no formation for attack when they advanced towards VAN HYCK FMR. Some wore steel helmets, some soft caps, all wore greatcoats, none wore equipment and many had no rifles. They were easily dispersed with Lewis Gun and rifle fire and their casualties are estimated at about 40.

The Battalion on the left apparently experienced serious difficulties and it was not possible to secure touch with it. The Battalion on the right continued to advance after our line was held up at 6-30 a.m. and apparently reached the first objective, but being unable to hold the position withdrew to their original front line. Unfortunately in the withdrawal heavy casualties were inflicted by enemy Machine Gun fire.

Communication with Battalion Headquarters was almost impossible by runners owing to the enemy sniping, and many runners were shot down in attempting to get back with reports. Communication by Lucas Lamps was not secured owing either to destruction of the apparatus by shell fire or to casualties amongst signallers. Of the pigeons taken forward, 4 were killed and 2 utilised. Telephonic Communication was maintained only with the Battalion on the left.

The ground over which the troops advanced was badly cut up by shell fire, and all shellholes were full of water. The going was very difficult and before the day was far advanced Lewis Guns and Rifles were rapidly becoming useless despite the use of breech covers. Heavy rain commenced to fall about mid-day.

The Right and Left flanks were in the air with the exception of a small flank party on the left; most of the Lewis Guns and rifles were out of action owing to the mud and the men were reduced in numbers and much exhausted through exposure and through being in waterlogged shell craters for 3 days and 2 nights. For the above reasons it was considered necessary to withdraw to the original line and this was effected by 5 p.m. During the withdrawal most of the wounded men were brought back into our lines.

Our casualties were:-

	Offrs.	O. R.
Killed.	2.	65.
Wounded.	3.	151.
Wounded (At DUTY.)	1.	7.
M. Y. D.	1.	7.
Missing.		48.
Wounded & Missing.		27.

Carlyel Harford
Lieut - Col.,
20/10/17.   Comndg. 4/5th Bn. L. N. Lancashire Regt.

Headquarters,
170th Infantry Brigade.

Answers to questions, Reference B.M.3761 d. 26/10/17.

1. The taping out of the forming up line was done by Compass.

2. The Battalion formed up on the Forming up Line by -

    1. Withdrawing Reserve platoon for 1st Wave.
    2. Withdrawing 2 Support platoons for Mopping up and 2nd Wave.
    3. Withdrawing Front Line platoon for 3rd Wave.

   No difficulties were experienced.

3. Direction of advance was kept by Compass.

4. The 1st Wave was 25 to 50 yards from the Barrage at the 1st jump.

5. Casualties were caused by enemy Machine Gun fire on reaching our original Front Line.

6. Our Barrage was quite close enough to our Forming up Line.
   No enemy were encountered between the Barrage Line and the Forming Up Line.

7. The Barrage was very good but rather too fast. It would have been better at 5 minutes per 50 yards. The jumps were not too big.

8. Rifle Covers and Muzzle Protectors were kept on until the rifles were used. Despite this, mud got in between the barrel and cover, in many cases. Most of the rifles were usable on removing the covers; subsequently, rifles gradually became unserviceable. Canvas Covers (full length and working parts) were used on the Lewis Guns.
   Eventually the guns became unusable.

9. No information available respecting the value of cords attached to Lewis Guns, as no guns were dropped in shell holes.

[signature]

30/10/17.

Lieut-Coln,
Commdg. 4/5th Bn. L. N. Lancs. Regt.

1:10 000   K.I.   Parts of 20 S.W. 4 / 20 S.E. 3   EDITION 2.

Message Pad.

Your Message must be such as will enable the Addressee to know what the Situation is with You and your Neighbours.

NEGATIVE INFORMATION IS ALSO VALUABLE.

Strike out and alter sentences as necessary.

TO ....

1. Am advancing to..
2. Am putting out (Have put out) protective parties.
3. Am sending out. Have sent out and am keeping out patrols to keep touch with the enemy.
4. Am (Have) consolidating (ed).
5. Our line now runs..
6. I require (give article or articles and number required) :—

   Send the above to..
7. Troops on my right are (give situation).

8. Troops on my left are (give situation)

9. My strength now is..
10. Am being shelled from..
11. Am held up by M.G., T.M., rifle, artillery fire from..................
12. Am now ready to..
13. Enemy line runs..
14. Enemy (strength)..at................
    doing..
15. Have captured..
16. Enemy prisoners belong to..
17. Enemy counter-attack forming up at..
18. Other remarks—

Time a.m. (p.m.)	Name..................................
Date..................................	Rank..................................
Place..................................	Platoon.............. Company..............
(Map Ref. or mark on back of map).	Battalion..................................

~~Compositions~~ ~~£2.9~~

Headquarters
127th Division

Herewith War Diary for the
Battalion under my Command,
period 1/11/17 to 30/11/17.

P.W. Kipps
Lt a/a/ [?] Lieut Col.
30/11/17.   Commdg. 2/5 N. Lancashire Regt.

WAR DIARY
of
INTELLIGENCE SUMMARY

Army Form C. 2118.

Place	Date	Hour	Summary of Events and Information	Remarks and references to Appendices
PROVEN	1/11/17		CAMP. Training	
"	2/11/17		" 1 Platoon to BOESINGHE as Carrying party for R.F.A	
"	3/11/17		" " " " " " " "	
"	4/11/17		" " " " " " " "	
"	5/11/17		" " " " " " " "	
"	6/11/17		" " " " " " " "	
"	7/11/17		" Carrying party for R.F.A. returned	
"	8/11/17		" Entrained at PROVEN Detrained at AUDRUICQ. Marched to LICQUES.	
LICQUES	9/11/17		LICQUES. Resting. Cleaning up. Reinforcements 1 off + 25 O.R.	
"	10/11/17		" do	
"	11/11/17		" Sunday	
"	12/11/17		" Training - Company	
"	13/11/17		" " Reinforcements 70 O.R.	
"	14/11/17		" "	

WAR DIARY
INTELLIGENCE SUMMARY
(Erase heading not required.)

Army Form C. 2118.

Instructions regarding War Diaries and Intelligence Summaries are contained in F. S. Regs., Part II. and the Staff Manual respectively. Title pages will be prepared in manuscript.

Place	Date	Hour	Summary of Events and Information	Remarks and references to Appendices
LICQUES	15/11/17		Training. Reinforcements 14 O.R.	
"	16/11/17		" Battalion Route March	
"	17/11/17		" Battalion Attack	
"	18/11/17		(Sunday)	
"	19/11/17		Training - Company & Individual	
"	20/11/17		" Battalion Attack	
"	21/11/17		" Company & Individual	
"	22/11/17		" Company & Battalion Attack	
"	23/11/17		" Company & Individual	
"	24/11/17		Bn. Route March	a.a.P
"	25/11/17		Sunday	a.a.P
"	26/11/17		Training A & B Coy Musketry C & D Coy Route March	a.a.P
"	27/11/17		" Company & Attachment	a.a.P
"	28/11/17		" C & D Coy Musketry A & B Coys Practice	a.a.P
"	29/11/17		" Battalion Attack. Transport Bomb Ccy	a.a.P
"	30/11/17		" A & C Coys Route March B & D Coy Musketry	a.a.P

Extract from 57th (West Lancs.) Divisional Routine Order No.1754, dated 27th November, 1917:-

HONOURS & AWARDS.

Under authority delegated by the Field Marshal-Commanding-in-Chief, the Corps Commander XIX Corps, has awarded decorations to the undermentioned N.C.O's and men for gallantry and devotion to duty in action:-
(Athy:- XIX Corps Routine Order No.935, dated 24/11/17.)

MILITARY MEDAL.

4/5th Bn. L. N. Lancashire Regiment.

242570,	Sgt. S. Heaton.	242562,	Sgt. P. Foster.
242672,	" J.S. Smith.	242532,	Cpl. G. Aspinall.
243366,	Pte. (A/Cpl) W. Wardle.	243172,	Pte.(L/Cpl) L. Cummins.
13989,	Pte. (L/Cpl) J. Hodgson.	243476,	do W. Hamer.
243312,	Pte. J. Berry.	244772,	Pte. F. Dean.
243561,	Pte. W. Hardacre.	242879,	Pte. R. Brabin.
244939,	Pte. A. Greenwood.	242864,	Pte. A. Coward.
243249,	Pte. C. Marsden.	16197,	Pte. S. Entwhistle
243522,	Pte. J. Crompton.	30212,	Pte. H. Halliwell.
	242467, Pte. J. Stevens.		

CERTIFIED true extract.

                                                    Lieut.,
                                                    A/Act.,
30/11/17.   4/5th Bn. L. N. Lancashire Regiment.

Headquarters
66th Division

Herewith War Diary of the
Battalion under my command,
period 1/12/17 to 31/12/17

[signature] Lieut. Col.
1.1.18. Commdg 2/5 E. Lancashire Regt.

9/11

Fortification

War Diary
of
4th Battalion Royal North Lancaster Regiment
From 1st December 1914 to 31st December 1917.
Volume II.

WAR DIARY
INTELLIGENCE SUMMARY

Army Form C. 2118.

(Erase heading not required.)

Place	Date	Hour	Summary of Events and Information	Remarks and references to Appendices
LICQUES	1st		Training. Battalion Route March. 2 Other Ranks struck off strength	A.P.
-do-	2nd		-do- Battalion Church Parade. Draft of 4 Other Ranks	A.P.
-do-	3rd		-do- Company Training. Draft of 2 Other Ranks	A.P.
-do-	4th		-do- Company Route March and Company Training	A.P.
-do-	5th		-do- Attack Practice and Company Training	A.P.
-do-	6th		-do- Company Training and Battalion Ceremonial Drill	A.P.
-do-	7th		-do- Brigade Attack Practice. 4 Other Ranks struck off strength	A.P.
-do-	8th		-do- Company Training. 4 Other Ranks struck off strength	A.P.
-do-	9th		-do- Battalion Tactical Schemes. Battalion marched at LICQUES and proceeded to PROVEN by Motor Lorries. Encamped at PUTLOWES CAMP at 6.30 p.m.	A.P.
PROVEN	10		Cleaning up of Camp and Commencing things Indications. One other rank proceed to England (Candidate for Commission)	A.P.
PROVEN	11		Company Training	A.P.
-do-	12		Company Training	A.P.
-do-	13		Battalion vacated PUTLOWES Camp and proceeded by March route to billets ROUSBRUGGE - HARINGE arrived 11.30 a.m.	A.P.

WAR DIARY
or
INTELLIGENCE SUMMARY.
(Erase heading not required.)

Army Form C. 2118.

Place	Date	Hour	Summary of Events and Information	Remarks and references to Appendices
ROUSBRUGGE - HARRINGE	14		Cleaning Arms Equipment & Billets	
do	15		Battalion Church Parade	
do	16		Vacated billets and proceeded by route march to St. WITTE CAMP WOESTEN Arrived at 11.5 am	
WOESTEN	17		Cleaning up and settling down in Camp	
"	18		Working parties on line under supervision of R.E.'s Tunnelling Co	
"	19		do	
"	20		do	
"	21		2 working parties on line. Remainder front march. route march to Training activities	
"	22		do	
"	23		do Training activities	
"	24		do	
"	25		Xmas Day Divine Service	
"	26		Working parties on line under supervision of R.E.s Tunnelling Co 2 Casualties	
"	27		do do	
"	28		do	

Army Form C. 2118.

WAR DIARY
or
INTELLIGENCE SUMMARY.
(Erase heading not required.)

Place	Date	Hour	Summary of Events and Information	Remarks and references to Appendices
DE WIPPE }	1917		Working parties supplies under supervision of R.E.'s travelling to	
WOESTEN	29			
	30		Sunday - Church Service	
	31		March to PROVEN to PRIVET CAMP PROVEN	

Confidential

Headquarters
57th Division

Herewith War Diary of the
Unit under my command, period 1st to
31st January 1918.

C. Lloyd Harford
Lieut-Col.
1.2.18.   Commdg. 4/5 L.L. Lancashire Regt.

Confidential.

War Diary
of
4th Battalion Royal North Lancashire Regiment.
From 1st January 1918 to 31st January 1918.
Volume 12.

WAR DIARY
or
INTELLIGENCE SUMMARY.
(Erase heading not required.)

Army Form C. 2118.

Instructions regarding War Diaries and Intelligence Summaries are contained in F. S. Regs., Part II. and the Staff Manual respectively. Title pages will be prepared in manuscript.

Place	Date 1918	Hour	Summary of Events and Information	Remarks and references to Appendices
	JAN.			
PROVEN	1		Resting at PRIVET CAMP	
"	2		Entrained at PROVEN detrained at STEENWERCK + went to camp there	
STEENWERCK	3		Marched to ERQUINGHEM and relieved the 41st Batt. Australian Imperial Force in Support Battalion of the CHAPELLE SECTOR	
ERQUINGHEM	4		Billets - 2 Companies in ERQUINGHEM + 2 Companies at LA ROLANDERIE FARME. cleaning up + training	
"	5		Working Parties + training	
"	6		Sunday - Batt. Church Service	
"	7		Working Parties + training	
"	8		do. Batt. Lewis Gun Section relieved	
"	9		L.G. Section in CHAPELLE sector.	
CHAPELLE SECTOR	10		Relieved 1st Kings Own (T.C.L) Regt in CHAPELLE Sector. E. Artillery active in morning. Overnight 2 patrols sent out (T 21 a 95.80) Enemy driven off. Having one wounded. Prisoner in our hands who on hand in our own line	

WAR DIARY
INTELLIGENCE SUMMARY

Army Form C. 2118.

Place	Date	Hour	Summary of Events and Information	Remarks and references to Appendices
CHAPELLE SECTOR	1918 Jan 11		Cloudy N.W. Very quiet day & night. Our patrols lay out during the night and listening parties went out to report enemy activity.	
	12		Considerably more enemy artillery in evidence. At night very quiet. Our patrols out during the night. Listening patrols to report the enemy movements. Enemy troughs - heavy then quiet then bursts of attack being ROMEO POST a silent raid then bombs (T 10 d 55.85). The hun signals on the 12" Sapphire line. The dropping of a smoke bomb with the Germans was mistaken by the Coy in command in POST. & This lot mistaken have par in the Post & C.S.M.'s and for respirators and on reaching Lieutenant & dragged them. attacked and out of the trench. The Corporal in command was also killed. Later he has all trenches was & bayonet. Whereupon the enemy withdrew. The	B

WAR DIARY
INTELLIGENCE SUMMARY

Army Form C. 2118.

Place	Date	Hour	Summary of Events and Information	Remarks and references to Appendices
CHAPELLE SECTOR	13		Corporal Unwin[?] put up a green Very light upon which the astonished L.G. post opened fire. The retaliatory enemy answered then captive and sentries subsequent search revealed 2 dead Boche but casualties were our own slightly wounded.	
			Slight visibility and great aerial activity on both sides. A quiet day with the exception of T.M. strafe J EVELYN POST vicinity from 6 am to 7.30 am (3 M.C.B + 6 min) of EVELYN POST (DAY POST) failed to report its arrival to Hdrs up its	
NAME OF SECTOR CHANGED K. "WEZ" MACQUART			night post at EYE. A search party was sent out to EVELYN + vicinity but no trace was found of them. Mini B.G. information or ammunition was obtained above the POST came under heavy T.M. + pineapple fire in the early morning.	

WAR DIARY of INTELLIGENCE SUMMARY

Army Form C. 2118.

(Erase heading not required.)

Instructions regarding War Diaries and Intelligence Summaries are contained in F. S. Regs., Part II. and the Staff Manual respectively. Title pages will be prepared in manuscript.

Place	Date 1919 JAN.	Hour	Summary of Events and Information	Remarks and references to Appendices
WEZ MACQUART SECTOR	14		Fall of snow in early morning. Quiet all day & night	
	15		Quiet all day. Relieved by 1st L.N. Lanc Regt and proceeded to ERQUINGHEM as RESERVE BATT.	
ERQUINGHEM	16		REST. Cleaning up	
"	17		BILLETS Working Parties up the line	
"	18		" do	
"	19		" Relieved 1st L.N. Lanc Regt	
WEZ MACQUART	20		Quiet all day & night. 2 Patrols out during night had nothing to report	
"	21		" do	
"	22		Quiet all day. Relieved by 1st L.N. Lanc Regt	
ERQUINGHEM	23		BILLETS - REST. Cleaning up	
"	24		" Working parties up the line	
"	25		" Relieved 1st L.N. Lanc Regt. Quiet during night	
WEZ MACQUART	26		Quiet during day & night. Patrols reported all quiet	
"	27		Very quiet all day & night. Patrols reported all quiet	
"	28		Snow fell. Visibility in spots not very good during day. All quiet	

WAR DIARY or INTELLIGENCE SUMMARY

Army Form C. 2118.

(Erase heading not required.)

Instructions regarding War Diaries and Intelligence Summaries are contained in F. S. Regs., Part II. and the Staff Manual respectively. Title pages will be prepared in manuscript.

Place	Date 1918 JAN	Hour	Summary of Events and Information	Remarks and references to Appendices
ERQUINGHEM	28		Relieved by 7th Royal N. Lancs. Regt.	
	29		BILLETS – First cleaning up howitzer trails	
	30		"	
	31		Relieved the 7th Royal N. Lancs. Regt. Under Scheme of alternative gun position of F/5 & D/5 – G.Ptlm + 252 after Rounds	
			returned ENERQUINGHEM	
				Officers 5th Rounds
			Batln. Stgth. 1st January 1918 36 659
			31st " (including 34 626 animals returned on 31/1/18)
			Distribution of New Year Honours.	
			BREVET MAJOR – Temp. Lt. Col. C. L. HAFORD (Cmdg. R. of 3. Sussex)	
			M.C. Capt Maj. B. H. KATERSON (Royal Munster Fusiliers)	
			M.M. III No 242507 Sjt. A. GRINSHAW	
			M.M. III No 29741 Cpl. W. GLOVER	

57TH DIVISION
170TH INFY BDE

2-5TH BN K.O.R OY. LANCASTER REGT.

~~6 FEB 1917 -~~

1915 AUG — 1916 FEB
and
1917 FEB — 1918 MAR
and
1919 JAN — 1919 MAY

www.ingramcontent.com/pod-product-compliance
Lightning Source LLC
Chambersburg PA
CBHW081443160426
43193CB00013B/2368